# PATTERNS

## Visual Perception Activities

## A Remedia Publication

**Written and illustrated by**
**Eleanor Villalpando**

REMEDIA PUBLICATIONS, INC. 10135 E. Via Linda, D124 Scottsdale, AZ 85258 1-800-826-4740

# Introduction

PATTERNS is a collection of activities to give children practice in recognizing and reproducing patterns.

It includes sequencing, reproducing simple designs and figures, peg and geo patterns, and grid designs. Through repeated practice in each area, children will build their skill level in determining position in space, shape discrimination, constancy of form, and pattern repetition. Difficulty level increases as children become more familiar with the tasks.

These reproducible worksheets will simplify your attempt to bridge the gap from concrete activities using blocks, pegs, and beads to the more abstract visual skills needed for reading and math.

The activities are such fun for children to do, they fail to realize the developmental growth being encouraged.

The activities in this book are perfect for use with pre-readers, primary children, and those needing remediation. Skill levels may be easily targeted and appropriate pages used.

**Look at each pattern row. Circle the shape that comes next.**

## Circle the shape that comes next.

**Circle the shape that comes next. Make the shape on the line.**

Name _____

**Circle the shape that comes next. Make the shape on the line.**

4

Name _____                    **SEQUENCE**

**Finish the pattern. Add the two shapes that would come next.**

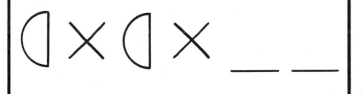 

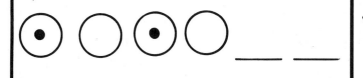 

**Look at each pattern. Circle the shape that comes next.**

**Circle the shape that comes next. Make the shape on the line.**

**Look at each pattern. Make the next shapes on the lines.**

△ ◯ △ △ ◯ ◯ △ △ ◯ ___ ___ ___

▢ ◦ ▢ ▢ ◦ ◦ ▢ ▢ ◦ ___ ___ ___

⊓ ▭ ⊓ ⊓ ▭ ▭ ⊓ ▭ ___ ___ ___

▽ △ ▽ ▽ △ △ ▽ △ ___ ___ ___

✕ ◯ ✕ ◯ ✕ ◯ ___ ___ ___

∪ ◯ ∪ ◯ ◯ ∪ ◯ ___ ___ ___

◇ ▯ ◇ ▯ ◇ ▯ ___ ___ ___

＋ △ ＋ △ ＋ △ ___ ___ ___

**Look at the pattern. Finish the row.**

Row 1: □ △ ○ □ △ ○ □ ___ ___ ___

Row 2: U → ▯ U → ▯ U ___ ___ ___

Row 3: ○ ○ ∘ ◯ ○ ∘ ◯ ___ ___ ___

Row 4: ▽ ✕ ✕ ▽ ✕ ✕ ▽ ___ ___ ___

Row 5: ▫ ◯ ▫ ▫ ◯ ▫ ▫ ___ ___ ___

Row 6: ⌂ + △ ⌂ + △ ⌂ ___ ___ ___

Row 7: ◖ ○ ◗ ◖ ○ ◗ ◖ ___ ___ ___

Row 8: ↑ △ □ ↑ △ □ ↑ ___ ___ ___

Name _____

**Finish each pattern.**

□ ▫ ○ △ □ ▫ ○ △ __ __ __ __

∩ ○ ○ □ ∩ ○ ○ □ __ __ __ __

◯ C △ □ ◯ C △ □ __ __ __ __

× × ○ △ × × ○ △ __ __ __ __

 __ __ __ __

 __ __ __ __

△ △ × ○ △ △ × ○ __ __ __ __

L U || □ L U || □ __ __ __ __

# What's missing?

Fill in the spaces in each pattern.

# What's missing?
**Fill in the spaces in each pattern.**

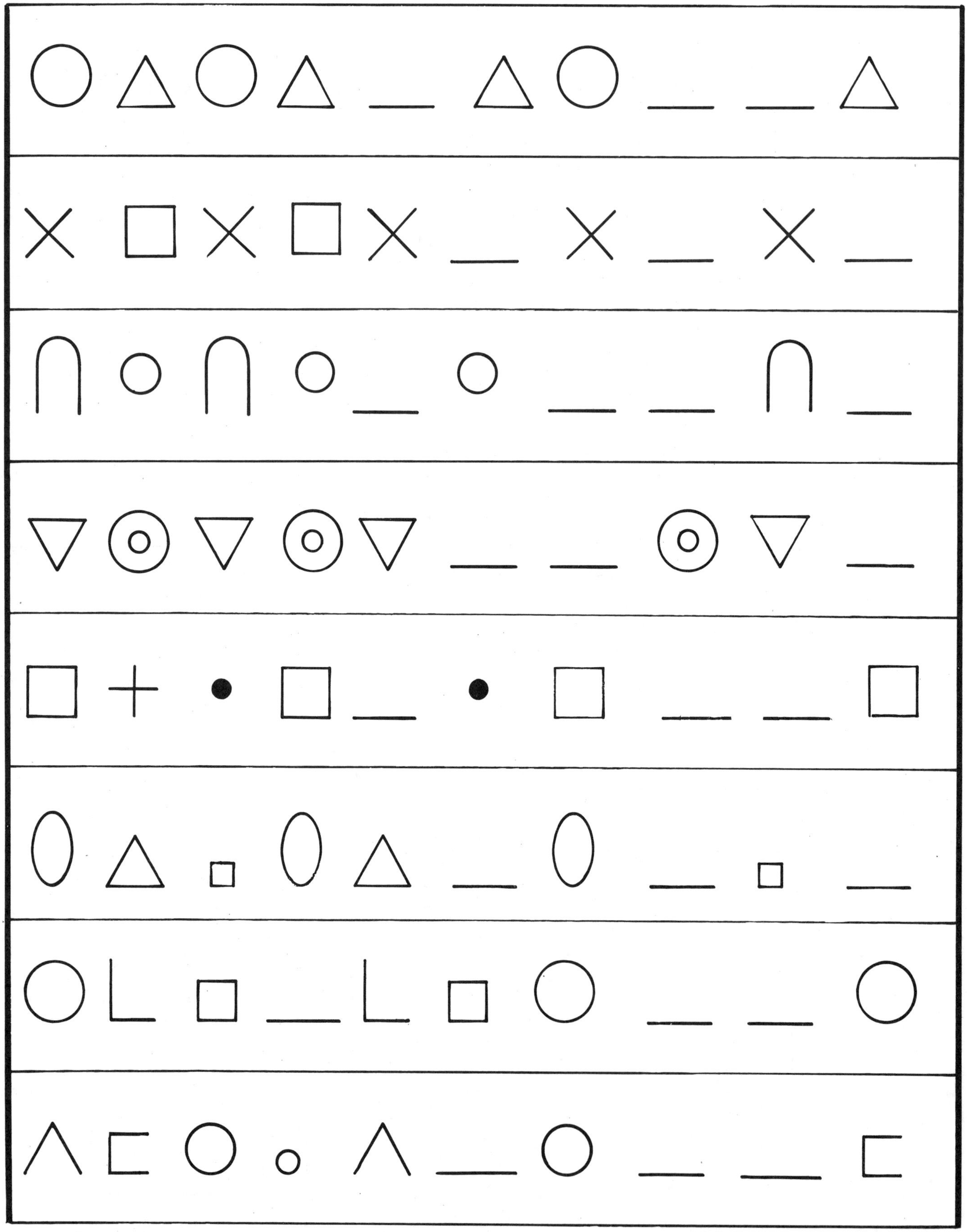

○ △ ○ △ _ △ ○ _ _ △

✕ □ ✕ □ ✕ _ ✕ _ ✕ _

∩ ○ ∩ ○ _ ○ _ _ ∩ _

▽ ⊙ ▽ ⊙ ▽ _ _ ⊙ ▽ _

□ + • □ _ • □ _ _ □

○ △ ▫ ○ △ _ ○ _ ▫ _

○ L □ _ L □ ○ _ _ ○

∧ ⊏ ○ ∘ ∧ _ ○ _ _ ⊏

**These shapes follow a pattern.**

**Which of these fits the pattern? Circle it.**

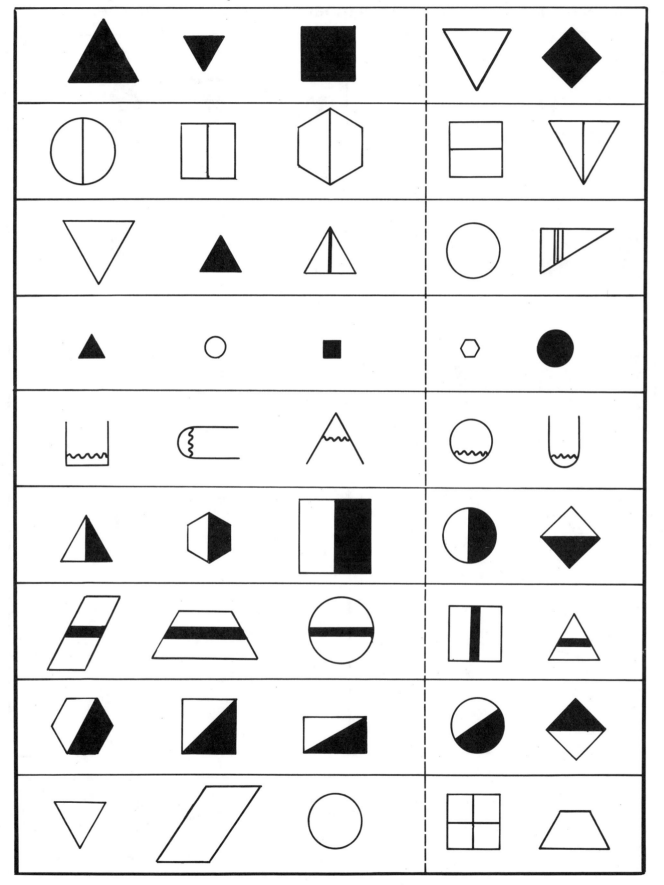

Name _____

**The shapes in each box follow a pattern. Choose the shape at the bottom that would fit the same pattern. Write the number of the shape on the line.**

**Make color patterns. Use two colors.**

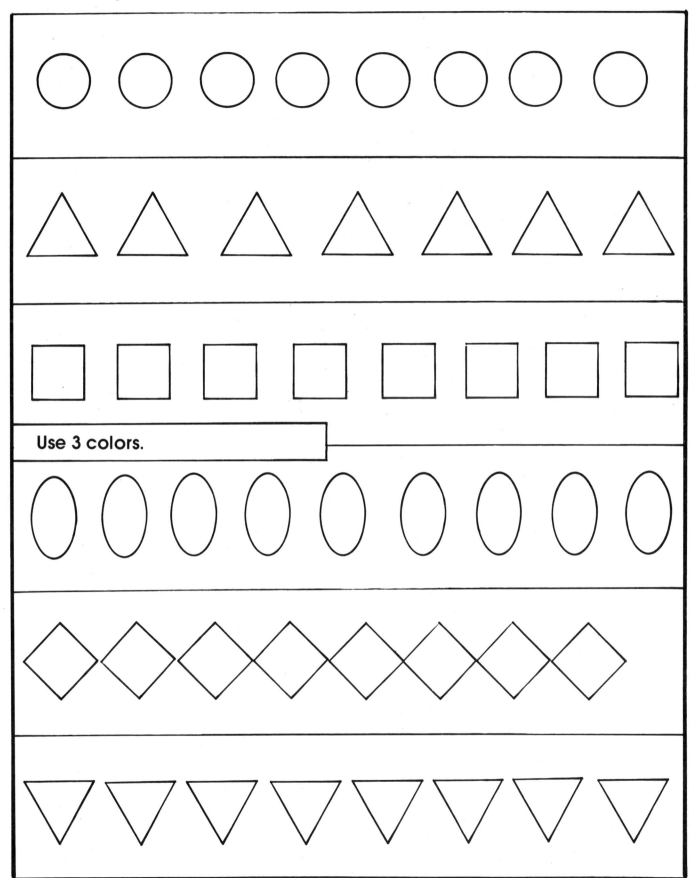

Use 3 colors.

**Finish each pattern.**

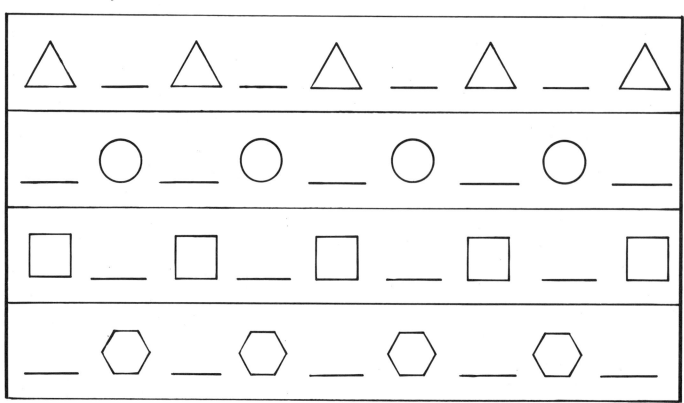

Choose three shapes. Make your own patterns. Use different shapes for each pattern.

○ □ ✕ ∪ △ ● T ◇ ◉ +

**Here is the pattern.**

**Which one comes next? Circle it.**

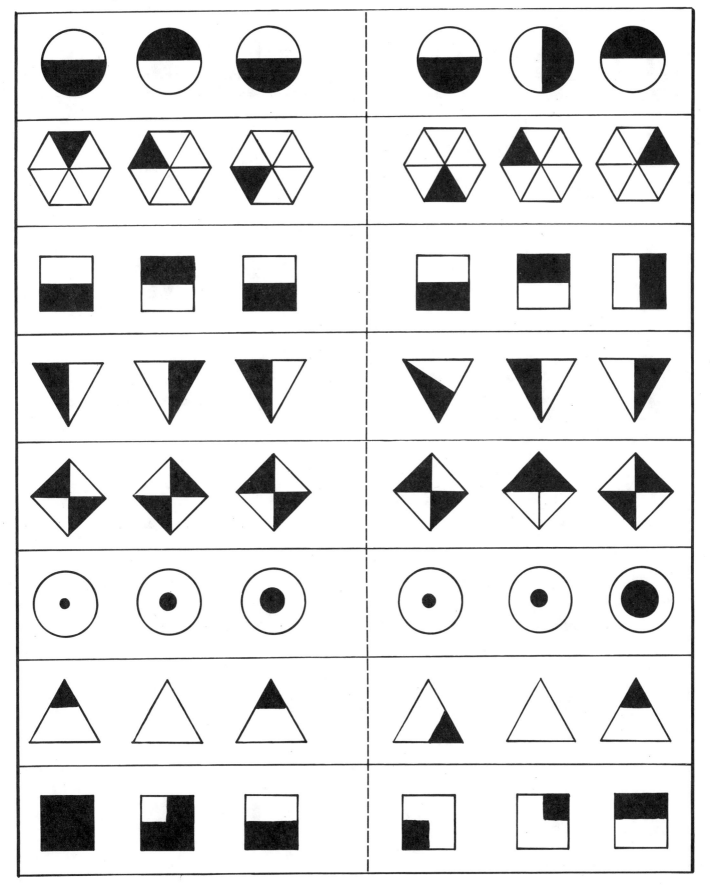

**Look at each pattern. Make the blank shape follow the pattern.**

**Make a row of each shape.**

| | | | |
|---|---|---|---|
| ◇ | | | |
| ◯△ | | | |
| ▢ | | | |
| ◯ | | | |
| ⌂ | | | |
| △ | | | |

**Make a row of each shape.**

**Circle the shapes used to make the one in the first box.**

Circle the shapes used to make the one in the first box. Then draw the first shape in the empty box.

## Draw the pictures.

## Draw the pictures.

## Draw the pictures.

## Draw these pictures.

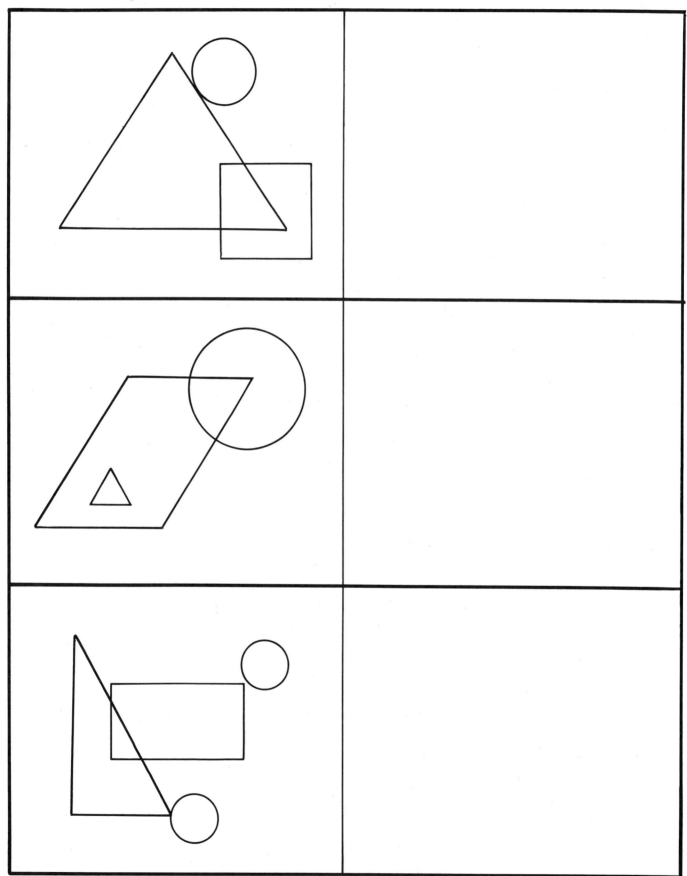

Name _____

Look at the dot patterns.

Make the same pattern in the box next to each one.

27

Name _____

**Look at the dot patterns.**

**Make the same pattern in the box next to each one.**

Name _____

**Look at the dot patterns.**

**Make the same pattern in the box next to each one.**

29

Name _____

**Look at the dot patterns.**

**Make the same pattern in the box next to each one.**

Name _____

**Make color patterns. Use the number code for the colors.**

1 - red    2 - blue    3 - yellow    4 - green

| | | | | |
|---|---|---|---|---|
| 3 | 2 | 1 | 2 | 3 |
| 3 | 2 | 1 | 2 | 3 |
| 1 | 1 | 1 | 1 | 1 |
| 3 | 2 | 1 | 2 | 3 |
| 3 | 2 | 1 | 2 | 3 |

| | | | | |
|---|---|---|---|---|
| 1 | 3 | 2 | 3 | 2 |
| 1 | 3 | 4 | 3 | 4 |
| 1 | 3 | 2 | 3 | 1 |
| 4 | 3 | 4 | 3 | 1 |
| 2 | 3 | 2 | 3 | 1 |

| | | | | |
|---|---|---|---|---|
| 3 | 4 | 2 | 4 | 3 |
| 4 | 3 | 2 | 3 | 4 |
| 2 | 2 | 4 | 2 | 2 |
| 4 | 3 | 2 | 3 | 4 |
| 3 | 4 | 2 | 4 | 3 |

| | | | | |
|---|---|---|---|---|
| 4 | 3 | 3 | 3 | 4 |
| 2 | 4 | 1 | 4 | 2 |
| 2 | 1 | 1 | 1 | 2 |
| 2 | 4 | 1 | 4 | 2 |
| 4 | 3 | 3 | 3 | 4 |

| | | | | |
|---|---|---|---|---|
| 3 | 3 | 1 | 1 | 1 |
| 3 | 3 | 4 | 4 | 1 |
| 1 | 4 | 3 | 4 | 1 |
| 1 | 4 | 4 | 3 | 3 |
| 1 | 1 | 1 | 3 | 3 |

**Make your own.**

| | | | | |
|---|---|---|---|---|
| ○ | ○ | ○ | ○ | ○ |
| ○ | ○ | ○ | ○ | ○ |
| ○ | ○ | ○ | ○ | ○ |
| ○ | ○ | ○ | ○ | ○ |
| ○ | ○ | ○ | ○ | ○ |

Name _____

Make color patterns. Choose the colors for each number. Write the color word on the line.

1. _____  3. _____

2. _____  4. _____

② ② ③ ① ①
② ③ ② ③ ①
③ ② ① ② ③
① ③ ② ③ ②
① ① ③ ② ②

④ ① ① ① ④
② ③ ③ ③ ②
② ③ ④ ③ ②
② ③ ③ ③ ②
④ ① ① ① ④

③ ② ① ② ③
② ① ④ ① ②
③ ④ ④ ④ ③
② ① ④ ① ②
③ ② ① ② ③

① ④ ③ ② ①
② ① ④ ③ ②
③ ② ① ④ ③
④ ③ ② ① ④
① ④ ③ ② ①

## Make your own color patterns.

○ ○ ○ ○ ○
○ ○ ○ ○ ○
○ ○ ○ ○ ○
○ ○ ○ ○ ○
○ ○ ○ ○ ○

○ ○ ○ ○ ○
○ ○ ○ ○ ○
○ ○ ○ ○ ○
○ ○ ○ ○ ○
○ ○ ○ ○ ○

Look at the pattern in each box.

Make the same pattern in the box beside each one.

33

Name _____

**Look at the pattern in each box.**

**Make the same pattern in the box beside each one.**

Name _____

Look at the pattern in each box.

Make the same pattern in the box beside each one.

Name _____

**Look at the pattern in each box.**

**Make the same pattern in the box beside each one.**

Can you make these pictures? Connect the dots carefully.

# More pictures!   Watch those dots!

# This is not easy!   Make the design in the box next to it.

## Make the blank grid look like the one next to it.

**Make the blank grid look like the one next to it.**

## Make the blank grid look like the one next to it.

**Make the blank grid look like the one next to it.**

**Make the blank grid look like the one next to it.**

**Make the blank grid look like the one next to it.**

## Choose two colors to make these patterns.